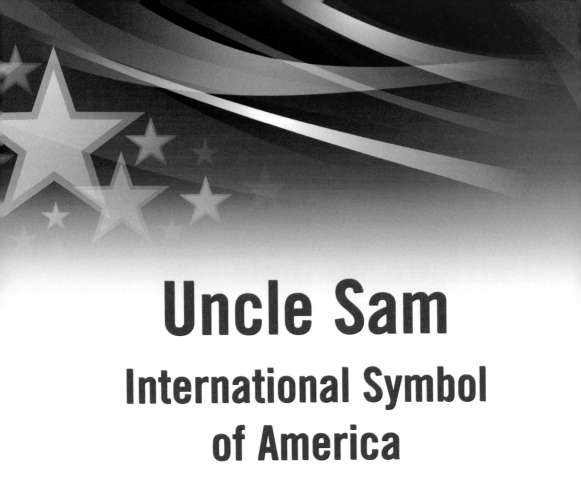

Uncle Sam

International Symbol of America

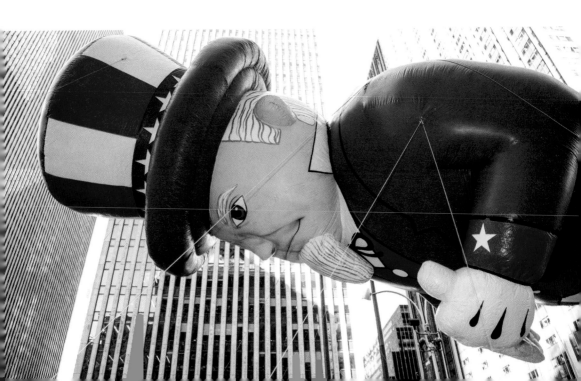

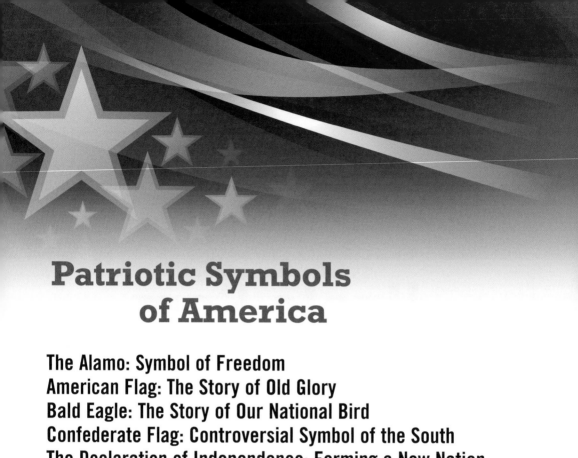

Patriotic Symbols
of America

The Alamo: Symbol of Freedom
American Flag: The Story of Old Glory
Bald Eagle: The Story of Our National Bird
Confederate Flag: Controversial Symbol of the South
The Declaration of Independence: Forming a New Nation
Ellis Island: The Story of a Gateway to America
Independence Hall: Birthplace of Freedom
Jefferson Memorial: A Monument to Greatness
Liberty Bell: Let Freedom Ring
Lincoln Memorial: Shrine to an American Hero
Mount Rushmore: Memorial to Our Greatest Presidents
The Pledge of Allegiance: Story of One Indivisible Nation
Rock 'n' Roll: Voice of American Youth
The Star-Spangled Banner: Story of Our National Anthem
Statue of Liberty: A Beacon of Welcome and Hope
Uncle Sam: International Symbol of America
The U.S. Constitution: Government by the People
Vietnam Veterans Memorial: Remembering a Generation and a War
Washington Monument: Memorial to a Founding Father
The White House: The Home of the U.S. President

Uncle Sam
International Symbol of America

Hal Marcovitz

Mason Crest
Philadelphia

Mason Crest
450 Parkway Drive, Suite D
Broomall, PA 19008
www.masoncrest.com

Printed and bound in the United States of America.

CPSIA Compliance Information: Batch #PSA2014. For further information, contact Mason Crest at 1-866-MCP-Book.

Publisher's note: all quotations in this book come from original sources, and contain the spelling and grammatical inconsistencies of the original text.

First printing
1 3 5 7 9 8 6 4 2

Library of Congress Cataloging-in-Publication Data

on file at the Library of Congress

ISBN: 978-1-4222-3135-7 (hc)
ISBN: 978-1-4222-8758-3 (ebook)

Patriotic Symbols of America series ISBN: 978-1-4222-3117-3

Contents

Patriotic Symbols and American History   **6**
Introduction by Barry Moreno

1. Lexington and Concord   **9**

2. Uncle Sam Comes to Troy   **13**

3. The Most Famous Poster   **23**

4. Uncle Sam the Salesman   **33**

5. An Enduring Symbol   **37**

Chronology   **42**

Series Glossary of Key Terms   **43**

Further Reading   **45**

Internet Resources   **45**

Index   **46**

KEY ICONS TO LOOK FOR:

 Text-dependent questions: These questions send the reader back to the text for more careful attention to the evidence presented there.

 Words to understand: These words with their easy-to-understand definitions will increase the reader's understanding of the text, while building vocabulary skills.

 Series glossary of key terms: This back-of-the book glossary contains terminology used throughout this series. Words found here increase the reader's ability to read and comprehend higher-level books and articles in this field.

 Research projects: Readers are pointed toward areas of further inquiry connected to each chapter. Suggestions are provided for projects that encourage deeper research and analysis.

 Sidebars: This boxed material within the main text allows readers to build knowledge, gain insights, explore possibilities, and broaden their perspectives by weaving together additional information to provide realistic and holistic perspectives.

Patriotic Symbols
and American History

Symbols are not merely ornaments to admire—they also tell us stories. If you look at one of them closely, you may want to find out why it was made and what it truly means. If you ask people who live in the society in which the symbol exists, you will learn some things. But by studying the people who created that symbol and the reasons why they made it, you will understand the deepest meanings of that symbol.

The United States owes its identity to great events in history, and the most remarkable of our patriotic symbols are rooted in these events. The struggle for independence from Great Britain gave America the Declaration of Independence, the Liberty Bell, the American flag, and other images of freedom. The War of 1812 gave the young country a song dedicated to the flag, "The Star-Spangled Banner," which became our national anthem. Nature gave the country its national animal, the bald eagle. These symbols established the identity of the new nation, and set it apart from the nations of the Old World.

To be emotionally moving, a symbol must strike people with a sense of power and unity. But it often takes a long time for a new symbol to be accepted by all the people, especially if there are older symbols that have gradually lost popularity. For example, the image of Uncle Sam has replaced Brother Jonathan, an earlier representation of the national will, while the Statue of Liberty has replaced Columbia, a woman who represented liberty to Americans in the early 19th century. Since then, Uncle Sam and the Statue of Liberty have endured and have become cherished icons of America.

Of all the symbols, the Statue of Liberty has perhaps the most curious story, for unlike other symbols, Americans did not create her. She was created by the French, who then gave her to America. Hence, she represented not what Americans thought of their country but rather what the French thought of America. It was many years before Americans decided to accept this French goddess of Liberty as a symbol for the United States and its special role among the nations: to spread freedom and enlighten the world.

This series of books is valuable because it presents the story of each of America's great symbols in a freshly written way and will contribute to the students' knowledge and awareness of them. It it to be hoped that this information will awaken an abiding interest in American history, as well as in the meanings of American symbols.

—Barry Moreno,
librarian and historian
Ellis Island/Statue of Liberty National Monument

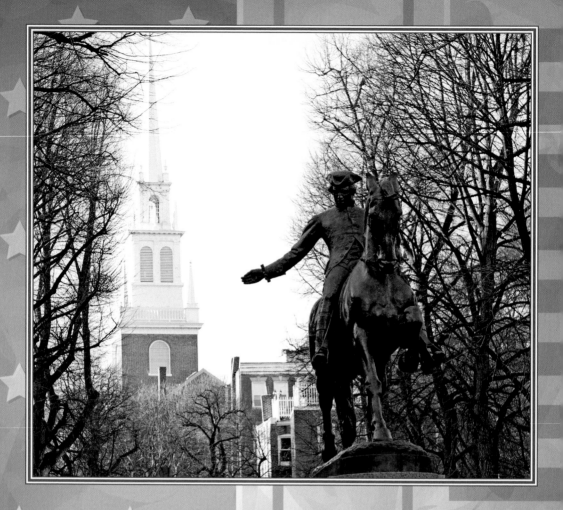

Words to Understand

militia—a fighting force of volunteers, usually organized by a state or local government.

minuteman—during the Revolutionary War, militia members who could be counted on to fight on short notice.

Revolutionary War—war fought between Great Britain and the American colonies from 1775 to 1783, ending with the independence of the United States of America. Also known as the American Revolution.

skirmish—a minor battle in a larger war.

This statue in Boston commemorates the April 1775 ride of Paul Revere to warn colonial villagers that the British Army was on its way. A young child named Sam Wilson was among the people who were awakened by Paul Revere; Sam would later become the basis for one of the most famous American symbols, Uncle Sam.

Lexington and Concord

Most school children are familiar with the story of Paul Revere, the American patriot whose ride across the Massachusetts countryside the night of April 18, 1775, warned colonists that 700 British soldiers under Lord General Hugh Percy were on the march.

As Revere rode down the Medford Road, his horse galloped through the tiny Massachusetts village of Arlington, which in 1775 was known as Menotomy. He passed a house where Edward and Lucy Wilson lived with their 13 children. One of those children was the Wilsons' eight-year-old son, Samuel.

A short distance up the road from Menotomy was the town of Lexington, where some 70 *minutemen* awaited the arrival of the British. Minutemen were members of the civilian *militia* in Massachusetts who volunteered "on a minute's notice" to defend the colony. The minutemen at Lexington were there to prevent British troops from seizing their store of gunpowder and ammunition.

The next morning, as the British troops approached Lexington, a small group became separated from Percy's main force and strayed into the village of Menotomy. The men of the town captured 18 British soldiers. These were first prisoners taken in the *Revolutionary War*. According to local legend, six of the British soldiers were so frightened of the Menotomy villagers that, in their haste to give themselves up, they found an old woman pulling dandelions and surrendered to her. The prisoners were soon turned over to the minutemen.

Later that morning, Lord Percy's soldiers met up with the 70 minutemen in Lexington. The fighting was brief. The minutemen were greatly outnumbered, but their heroism in the face of tremendous odds set the tone for the War for Independence that would follow.

"Stand your ground," the minutemen's captain, John Parker, told his troops. "Don't fire unless fired upon, but if they mean to have a war, let it begin here."

The British opened fire; eight minutemen were killed in the *skirmish* before the colonists retreated.

The British soldiers chased the minutemen back down Medford Road. Again, the war found its way to the streets of Menotomy. Here, a fierce battle raged. Edward Wilson joined many other residents of the town and minutemen in fighting against the British invaders.

Many townspeople lost their lives that day. Later, Hannah Winthrop of Boston wrote about what she saw. "We passed through the bloody field of Menotomy, which was strewn with mangled bodies," she wrote. "We met one affectionate father with a cart looking for his murdered son and picking up his neighbors who had fallen in battle in order for their burial."

A few hours later, about 200 minutemen regrouped at Concord, a short distance away. Again, they clashed with a superior force of British soldiers. But his time, the minutemen prevailed and drove the British out of Concord. Soon, the British soldiers were in retreat, chased all the way back to Boston by a fierce and dedicated force of American colonists.

Edward Wilson survived the fighting that day. So did his son. Sam Wilson had seen his father and his family's friends and neighbors fight for the cause of liberty and freedom. In the years to follow, Sam Wilson—in a truly unique way—would help light the fire of patriotism that burns in the hearts of millions of Americans.

Text-Dependent Questions
Who were the minutemen? Why did they come out to confront the British Army in Lexington during April 1775?

Research Project
The word *patriot* means a person who feels a strong love for and connection to their country. What are some things that you can do to show patriotism? How do most Americans react to patriotic displays and symbols?

Words to Understand

advertisement—a paid announcement, usually for goods and services for sale, that appears in newspapers and magazines.

Congress—the lawmaking branch of the American government.

contract—an agreement, whether written or spoken, between two or more people to provide goods or services.

morning coat—a formal jacket with long tails.

political cartoon—a drawing that uses humor or irony to make a statement about the government, its leaders, or its policies.

slaughterhouse—a place where cattle, pigs, chickens, turkeys, and other animals are butchered for their meat.

stockyard—an outdoor pen for animals, usually located next to a slaughterhouse.

This newspaper drawing of Uncle Sam sitting in a rocking chair dates to around 1830. It is one of the first images of the popular character. Over the years, Uncle Sam grew older and his characteristic white beard and star-spangled clothes were added.

Uncle Sam Comes to Troy

Most Americans, whether they are veterans of the armed services, children who laugh at a stilt-walker in an Independence Day parade, or readers of *political cartoons* in the newspapers, are familiar with the image of Uncle Sam: the elderly yet spry patriot with the white whiskers who favors top hats, striped pants, and *morning coats* decorated with the stars and stripes.

However, few Americans are aware that Uncle Sam owes his story to the customs of the meat packing business in upstate New York, and to a joke made by a *stockyard* worker.

The story begins in Mason, New Hampshire, where Edward and Lucy Wilson had moved their family after the Revolutionary War. Edward took up farming.

Sam Wilson, eight years old during the battles of Lexington and Concord, grew up on that New Hampshire farm in Mason. He also met his future wife in Mason. One of the town's residents was Benjamin Mann, who had been a captain in the Continental Army and veteran of the Battle of Bunker Hill. Captain Mann had a daughter named Betsey. In 1797 Sam Wilson and Betsey Mann were married.

But first, Sam would leave New Hampshire to find a job. In 1789, Sam and his brother, Ebenezer, left their father's farm and set out on foot for Troy, New York. This was a walk of some 150 miles.

Sam was 22 and Ebenezer 27 when they arrived in Troy and looked for work. They found jobs as brick-mak-

Captain Benjamin Mann of Mason, New Hampshire, had a nephew named John Chapman, who lived in nearby Lunenberg, Massachusetts. Years later, John Chapman became known as Johnny Appleseed, the pioneer who traveled throughout Ohio, Illinois, and Indiana planting apple orchards. It seems likely that Johnny Appleseed and the man who would serve as the inspiration for Uncle Sam were acquainted at least casually since they were, after all, related by marriage.

ers. It is likely that the Wilson brothers made many of the bricks that were used in Troy's earliest buildings, some of which are still standing today. One building that contained bricks made by the Wilson brothers was the city's first courthouse and jail.

> **Make Connections**
>
> After the Revolutionary War, citizens of the small towns throughout New York began naming their communities after ancient cities of Italy and Greece. Today, the cities of Rome, Utica, Syracuse, Ithaca, Delphi, and Troy can be found in New York state. The citizens of Troy had decided to rename their town just a few weeks before Sam and Ebenezer Wilson arrived. For years, the town had been known by the Dutch name Vanderheyden.

The Wilsons worked hard, and they soon had their own brick-making business. In 1793, Sam and Ebenezer went into the meatpacking business as well. They bought some land and built a *slaughterhouse* and dock on the Hudson River so they could load the barrels of beef and pork onto boats that sailed down the river for New York City and the other port towns on the Hudson. They also bought a farm near Troy.

And so Sam and Ebenezer settled into life as prosperous Troy businessmen. In 1797, Sam returned to Mason, where he married Betsey. They had four children, although two died young.

Many members of the Wilson and Mann families decided to follow Sam and Betsey back to Troy. They may have been drawn by the idea that Sam and Ebenezer would find a way to share their success with

Make Connections

Sam Wilson was born September 13, 1766; on that date in 1814, Francis Scott Key wrote the words that would become the "Star Spangled Banner" as he watched the British bombardment of Fort McHenry.

their relatives. Indeed they would. Several Manns and Wilsons found jobs at the meatpacking firm of E&S Wilson in Troy.

Within a short time, the Manns and Wilsons were two of Troy's most prominent and largest families. Since Sam had 12 brothers and sisters, the Manns and Wilsons provided Troy with many young children. That meant Sam Wilson had many nieces and nephews. There was no shortage of young children in Troy who could walk past the riverfront yard of E&S Wilson and see their Uncle Sam hard at work, tending to his business. In fact, it seemed that everybody in Troy started calling him "Uncle" Sam Wilson, regardless of whether they were related to him.

At E&S Wilson, business was brisk. The city of Troy grew in population in the first years of the 19th century. There was rich farmland nearby, and the town was lucky to be a port on the Hudson River, which was growing into one of the young nation's most important waterways. These things helped Troy grow. And as the town grew, so did the meatpacking firm of E&S Wilson.

But elsewhere in America, things were not so good. The British had never fully accepted their defeat at the hands of the colonists in the Revolutionary War.

Meanwhile, the British continued skirmishing with the French, their long-time enemies, particularly on the high seas. Britain needed sailors for its navy, so in 1802 English warships started kidnapping American sailors and forcing them into service. Next, the British openly attacked American ships sailing to France.

Members of *Congress,* including John Calhoun and Henry Clay, wanted the United States to fight back. They suggested attacks on Canada, which was ruled by England, and Florida, which at the time was owned by Spain, a British ally. Finally, on June 18, 1812, America declared war on Britain. The War of 1812 had begun.

Troy found itself very much involved in the war effort. The U.S. government bought 300 acres of land in Greenbush, New York, just south of Troy, and erected barracks for some 6,000 troops. The troops were placed under the leadership of General Henry Dearborn, who would lead the "Northern Expedition"—an attack on Canada. Dearborn intended to start the march north in the spring of 1813.

Somebody had to feed the troops. That job fell to a New York City businessman named Elbert Anderson, who won the government *contract* to supply beef and pork to all U.S. Army soldiers in New York and New

Make Connections

Troy, New York, doesn't consider Uncle Sam its only claim to fame; during the 1800s, many textile mills operated in the city. They had a widespread reputation for producing men's shirts with detachable collars.

Jersey. Anderson needed a lot of pork and beef to fulfill his contract, so he placed *advertisements* in several newspapers in search of packers capable of turning out dozens of barrels of meat a day.

Readers of New York newspapers were likely to see this advertisement, which had been placed by Anderson in October 1812:

VITAL FIGURE: Henry Dearborn

General Henry Dearborn, who led the troops camped just outside Troy, New York, was born in 1751 in Hampton, New Hampshire. He studied to be a physician, but left the practice of medicine during the Revolutionary War to serve as a captain in his state's militia. Dearborn and his men fought in the Battle of Bunker Hill.

Later, Dearborn was captured by the British, but rejoined the Continental Army after he was included in a prisoner exchange. He participated in the harsh encampment at Valley Forge, Pennsylvania, in 1777 with General George Washington. After the war, he settled in Maine, which he represented in Congress. He was secretary of war under President Thomas Jefferson.

When the War of 1812 broke out, Dearborn returned to active service, becoming a major general and leading the nation's Northern Expedition campaign against British troops in Canada. He met with mixed success, capturing Toronto and Fort George on the Niagara River, but losing Detroit to the British and suffering many losses at Sackett's Harbor, New York.

After the war, Henry Dearborn served as minister to Portugal. Fort Dearborn, a settlement in Illinois that was named in his honor, eventually grew into the city of Chicago.

Sealed proposals will be received through the medium of
the post offices at Albany and New York, directed to the
subscriber, until the 25th of October, for 2,000 barrels of
prime pork and 3,000 barrels of prime beef, to be delivered
in the months of January, February, March and April, at
Waterford, Troy, Albany and New York. The whole to be
put up in full bound barrels of white oak. Elbert Anderson,
Army Contractor.

E&S Wilson of Troy, New York, placed a bid and was
awarded the contract to provide General Dearborn's
troops at Greenbush with pork and beef.

Back in 1812, when food was shipped in barrels, it
was the practice of the meatpacker to stamp the initials
of the customer onto the lid of the barrel. And so, many
of the barrels stacked on the E&S Wilson dock on the
Hudson River carried this stamp: "E.A.–U.S.," meaning
the customers were Elbert Anderson and the United
States government.

One of the employees at E&S Wilson was Jonas W.
Gleason, a town character and prankster who enjoyed
making speeches at Independence Day picnics and
leading the Troy volunteer fire department. He was the
yard foreman at E&S Wilson. It was his job to make sure
the barrels got to the Hudson River dock, so they could
be sent to customers.

Somewhere around the spring of 1813 there was a
large shipment of barrels sitting on the dock, all stamped
with the initials "E.A.–U.S." A group of visitors wan-
dered by and saw the stamped barrels sitting on the

dock. They asked Gleason about what was in the barrels and the meaning of the initials.

Gleason replied that the barrels contained food for the soldiers, and that they were presently owned by his boss, Uncle Sam.

"Uncle Sam who?" asked one of the visitors.

"Why, Uncle Sam Wilson," Gleason answered. "It is he who is feeding the army."

Apparently, everybody had a good laugh at the joke, and the visitors were soon on their way. But they took the story with them, and word soon spread all over town that Uncle Sam Wilson was responsible for feeding the army of the United States. It was true, because Sam Wilson was responsible for providing food to General Dearborn's soldiers.

Around Troy, the joke never seemed to die. Soon, all government property in the Troy area was referred to as belonging to Uncle Sam. Wagons, mules, arms, ammunition—anything that was stamped "U.S." was said to belong to Uncle Sam. And since there was a camp of 6,000 soldiers just south of town, there were a lot of goods passing through Troy in those days stamped "U.S." Even the soldiers at Greenbush caught onto the joke; they started referring to their Army pay as coming from Uncle Sam.

Next, the local newspapers picked up the story. On September 7, 1813, the *Troy Post* published a story about the "border war"—General Dearborn's attack on

Canada—and how the success of the expedition "lights upon Uncle Sam's shoulders." Obviously, the newspaper wasn't talking about local meatpacker Sam Wilson, but how the federal government in Washington, now referred to as Uncle Sam, was responsible for ensuring a successful outcome of the war.

What did the real Uncle Sam Wilson think of all this? He was delighted, and never tired of telling people that he was the inspiration for what was fast becoming a symbol of America.

In 1917, Sam Wilson's great-nephew, Lucius Wilson, told this story:

> I was about 18 when Uncle Sam passed away. He was the old original Uncle Sam that gave the name to the United States. . . . he was jolly, genial, generous and known and called "Uncle Sam" by everyone. His wife was like him, widely known and called "Aunt Betsey." In my boyhood days I lived within half a dozen blocks of Uncle Sam. My father told me the Uncle Sam story and I have heard him tell it to others dozens of times.

Text-Dependent Question
Which members of Congress were leaders of the faction that wanted the United States to declare war on Great Britain in 1812, and to attack the British colony in Canada?

Research Project
The War of 1812 has often been called "the Second American Revolution." To explain this, you will need to research and understand the causes of this conflict, as well as what its resolution meant for the United States and its relationship with Great Britain.

Words to Understand

caricature—a drawing that humorously exaggerates the physical peculiarities of someone or something.

commentaries—written opinions on news and events published in newspapers and magazines.

communism—a form of government that is based on government ownership of all property, rather than ownership by individuals.

corruption—the illegal practice of government officials to accept money for favors.

Industrial Revolution—an era in America beginning in the mid-19th century that saw tremendous expansion in factory production.

politician—a person who seeks or holds public office.

tavern—in early America, a place where travelers could find food, drinks, and lodging.

Few people could argue with artist James Montgomery Flagg (pictured at left) when he boasted that his image of Uncle Sam was "the most famous poster in the world." The image originally appeared on the cover of *Leslie's* magazine (right), where it was spotted by military recruiters. More than 4 million copies of the army's "I Want You" posters were printed during World War I.

The Most Famous Poster

Following the War of 1812, the story of Uncle Sam grew into much more than just a local joke told in the *taverns* of Troy. Soon, people across America referred to their country and its government not by the true name, the United States, or by its initials, U.S., but by its adopted name: Uncle Sam.

Perhaps Uncle Sam came along when he was needed the most. By the War of 1812, the United States was still a young nation. It had been founded just 36 years before when the Declaration of Independence was signed in Philadelphia. There was no national image of America to serve as a symbol for the citizens. And, certainly, there were still people living in America who had questions about whether there should even be a United States government: they felt the states should have all the power.

On October 9, 1813, the newspaper *Columbian Centinel* of Boston suggested that volunteers from Vermont would do well to walk away from the Army because the federal government had failed to meet its obligations to pay the men. "The pretense is, that Uncle Sam does not pay well, and that the cold begins to pinch," the newspaper suggested.

So Uncle Sam seemed to be serving a number of purposes. He provided a figure of authority for the men of the army to look to for food, clothes, and pay, and he provided an image for newspaper editors to criticize when they wanted to complain about the government.

But what did Uncle Sam look like?

Although there was a real, live Uncle Sam—Sam Wilson of Troy lived until 1854—the Uncle Sam of folklore still did not have a face or body. That changed in 1830, when Uncle Sam showed up in an unsigned newspaper drawing titled "Uncle Sam in Trouble." The artist depicted Uncle Sam as a plump, sad fellow who is sitting down while President Andrew Jackson draws blood from an open vein in his arm. The drawing was a comment by the artist on Jackson's attempt to close down the Bank of the United States, a hot issue of the day.

The Uncle Sam of the 1830 newspaper cartoon hardly resembled the real Uncle Sam. Sam Wilson was tall and well-muscled. That newspaper artist in 1830 did show insight into the future in at least one way, though. In the drawing, he has pictured Uncle Sam dressed in a robe stitched out of an American flag.

An artist named Frank H. T. Bellow, took a crack at drawing Uncle Sam in 1854. Bellow's Uncle Sam was tall and skinny, and he appeared to need a haircut, shave, and bath. Also, his patriotic clothes are replaced by an ordinary top hat and coat with tails. This was not an image likely to become a symbol of American patriotism.

As the years went by, Uncle Sam kept showing up in cartoons; he became a character employed by the artists to illustrate their *commentaries* on the news of the day. America has a free press, a right guaranteed by the U.S. Constitution. That meant people were free to make fun of public officials, whether they were the local mayor or the president of the United States. Time and again, Uncle Sam found himself as a character in political cartoons. He was drawn old, young, thin, and plump. He wore star-spangled clothes in some drawings, ordinary street clothes in others.

At some point, Uncle Sam emerged in the shape and dress that most Americans would recognize today. That happened in the 1870s, when Thomas Nast started drawing him. Nast

Make Connections

One of Sam Wilson's descendants was William Henry Jackson, who would find fame as a photographer in the Old West. Later in life, Jackson took up oil painting. He produced portraits of his relatives by copying old paintings. "I'm sure that no one would ever recognize Uncle Sam, for my portrait showed him without the characteristic whiskers," Jackson said.

was the staff artist for *Harper's Weekly,* a very influential news and opinion magazine in the 1800s. In those days, photography was in its infancy; magazines and newspapers would not have the technical know-how to reproduce photographs in their pages until the 1920s. And so, editors turned to artists to illustrate the stories and commentaries in their publications.

One of Nast's first drawings of Uncle Sam was pub-

VITAL FIGURE: Thomas Nast

Cartoonist Thomas Nast was born in Germany in 1840, but moved to New York City with his family at the age of six. He found his first job as an artist at 15, when he was hired to provide drawings for *Frank Leslie's Illustrated Newspaper.* Soon, Nast was sent to Europe to produce drawings of radical changes taking place in European society—many of his sketches for American newspapers covered a revolt in Italy.

He returned to New York and a job at *Harper's Weekly* just in time for the Civil War. He was a vigorous opponent of slavery, and used his cartoons to promote the cause of abolition. This caused President Abraham Lincoln to call Nast "our best recruiting sergeant." Nast is also responsible for creating the symbols of the donkey for the Democratic Party and elephant for the Republican Party.

Following the war, he turned his attention to politics and corruption in New York City, using the power of his cartoons to help bring down William Marcy "Boss" Tweed and his political machine known as Tammany Hall. He soon fell on hard times, though. He lost all his money in the stock market and had a falling out with *Harper's Weekly* editors. He died in 1902 in Ecuador, where he had been sent by President Theodore Roosevelt to serve as the U.S. ambassador.

lished by *Harper's Weekly* in 1874. It showed a farmer about to dig up a mushroom labeled *"communism"* while Uncle Sam looks on in approval. This image shows a white-whiskered Uncle Sam in striped pants, long coat, star-spangled vest and top hat.

During the next few years, Nast continued to draw Uncle Sam as a rail-thin, aging patriot, sometimes bewildered by the antics of the local *politicians*, sometimes laughing at their errors. But there was no question about it: Nast's Uncle Sam was an American who represented the values and desires of Americans.

Nast never explained how he got the idea for his image of Uncle Sam, but many people believe he was inspired by a circus clown named Dan Rice.

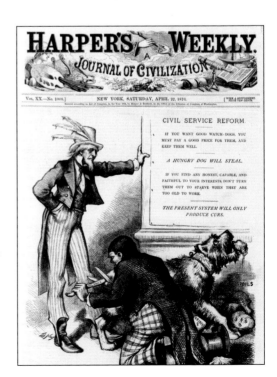

Thomas Nast was particularly effective at using his talent as an artist for biting social commentary. In this cartoon from the April 22, 1876, issue of *Harper's Weekly*, Nast shows Uncle Sam supporting civil service reform. Nast popularized the image of Uncle Sam as a tall, thin, older man wearing red, white, and blue clothing.

Make Connections

The largest statue of Uncle Sam can be found in Lake George, New York, where a 38-foot-tall fiberglass image of Uncle Sam has been erected in the parking lot of the Magic Forest amusement park. The statue weighs 4,500 pounds.

From the 1840s to the 1870s, Rice was the most famous clown in the United States. He toured with several circuses, winning fans and drawing large crowds in cities across America. Back then, the circus was a very important mode of entertainment for people. In those days there were no televisions, radios, or cinemas to provide people with excitement or laughs.

Rice joined his first circus in 1843 as a trick rider, but then developed an act with a trained pig he called "Lord Byron." He soon drifted from circus to circus, trying a number of different acts until 1848, when he settled in for life as a clown. By the 1850s, he was billing himself as "America's favorite clown."

In the 1860s, Rice developed a unique costume: he dressed in a stars-and-stripes coat with blue leotards, red-and-white trunks, a top-hat and long white whiskers. It is certainly likely that when the circus stopped off for a show in New York, a member of the audience was the cartoonist from *Harper's Weekly*, who found inspiration in the comic antics and dress of America's favorite clown.

And so Uncle Sam spent the rest of the 19th century as a character in political cartoons, or as a clown in the center ring of the circus. Although cartoonists continued to use Uncle Sam to represent the American will, many people believed the United States should not take an active part in international affairs. Following the Civil War, the *Industrial Revolution* provided new jobs for workers and contributed to the creation of bustling, busy cities. Americans were focused on issues at home.

But there were dark clouds on the horizon as the century passed. In Europe, royal families that had held power over their countries for centuries found themselves resisting calls to bring democracy to their subjects. In places like Russia, Germany, and Austria-Hungary,

---

VITAL FIGURE: Dan Rice

Every Uncle Sam stilt-walker who has marched in an Independence Day parade and every Uncle Sam impersonator who has taken a pie in the face at the circus can thank the clown Dan Rice for originating the idea of Uncle Sam as a comic. He was born Daniel McLaren Jr. in New York City on January 23, 1832. He was the stepson of a milkman, which means he grew up around horses. In the 1800s, all milk trucks were pulled by horses.

He learned to ride at an early age and was on his way to a career as a racehorse jockey, but at 17 he grew too heavy and had to find other work. McLaren found it at a circus. Over the years, he had learned some horse-riding stunts, and soon found himself in demand as a trick rider.

McLaren next tried an act with a trained pig before settling in for a career as a clown, using the stage name "Dan Rice." He became so popular that during a performance in Washington in 1850, Congress adjourned its business so that its members could catch his show. He continued performing in a number of circuses until 1887, then retired. He died in 1890.

the old kings refused to give in, and that led to war. World War I erupted in 1914, drawing much of Europe into conflict. The United States tried to stay out of the war, but in 1917 the need for America to come to the aid of its allies in Europe could no longer be ignored. America prepared to send its soldiers overseas.

As the War Department geared up for the conflict, the government realized it would need many soldiers. On July 6, 1916, the magazine *Leslie's Weekly* featured a portrait of Uncle Sam on its cover and the caption: "What Are You Doing for Preparedness?"

This Uncle Sam was no circus clown or cartoon *caricature.* True, he wore the familiar star-spangled hat,

This cartoon was published in September 1898, shortly after the end of the Spanish-American War. It shows Uncle Sam extending a hand to provinces freed from Spanish rule during the war: Cuba, Puerto Rico, and the Philippines.

James Montgomery Flagg's image of Uncle Sam was used on many different recruiting posters. This one from 1917 encourages Americans to enlist in the U.S. Navy.

blue overcoat and white whiskers, but this Uncle Sam was serious and stern. With a sharp brow, prominent nose, red-colored cheeks, and piercing eyes, the look on his face told it all. He seemed to be asking, "Are you ready for war?"

The poster had been drawn by illustrator James Montgomery Flagg. The magazine cover caught the eye of the War Department, which asked Flagg to adapt it to a recruiting poster for the armed forces. The poster Flagg produced showed the same image of Uncle Sam under the caption: "I Want You for the U.S. Army." More than 4 million of the posters were printed in 1917 and 1918, the two years America fought in World War I.

Text-Dependent Question

Who were some of the cartoonists who depicted Uncle Sam in newspapers or magazines during the 19th century?

Research Project

When World War I broke out in 1914, most Americans wanted to maintain an "isolationist" stance, in which the U.S. would not intervene on either side of the conflict. However, as the conflict expanded several things occurred that eventually forced American leaders to enter the war on the side of Britain, France, and their allies. Check out a book on World War I from your library, and identify three things that led the United States to end its isolationist approach.

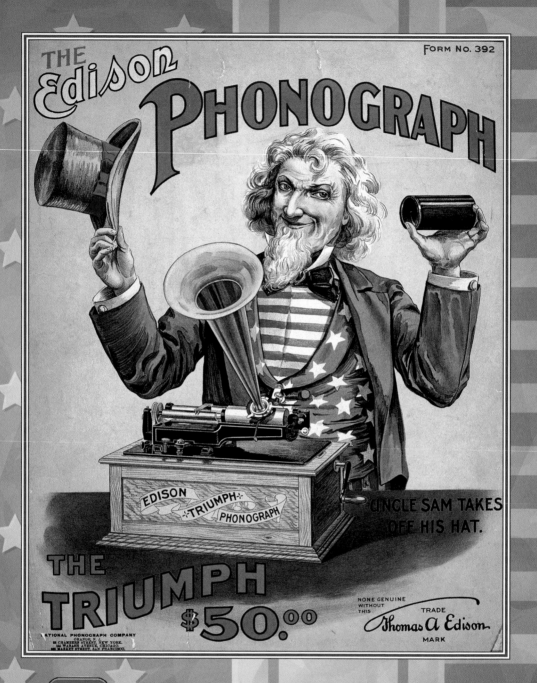

Words to Understand

commission—to appoint or assign a task to someone.
jingle—a short, catchy song, usually used for advertisements.

Uncle Sam pitches an early record player in this turn-of-the-century advertisement. Over the years, the image of Uncle Sam has been used to sell many different products, from alcohol to soap to motor oil. Even today, Uncle Sam appears on billboards and cereal boxes.

Uncle Sam the Salesman

It wasn't only the United States government that noticed Uncle Sam had an appeal to Americans. Early on, American corporations used the image of Uncle Sam in their advertisements to lure customers.

Among the first companies to use Uncle Sam as a pitchman was Berry Brothers, which manufactured hard oil finish for furniture. Berry's advertisements, which appeared in magazines in the early 1900s, portrayed Uncle Sam delivering boxes of the company's products to a group of anxious customers. The caption under the advertisement read: "Uncle Sam Supplying the World with Berry Brothers Hard Oil Finish."

The Wapato Fruit and Cold Storage Company of Wapato, Washington, used Uncle Sam to sell tomatoes.

Labels on the company's crates of tomatoes depicted a long-whiskered Uncle Sam holding his hat in his hand and gazing at a juicy, fresh-sliced tomato, as well as the words: "Uncle Sam Yakima Valley Tomatoes."

In 1903, Uncle Sam Shoemakers of Boston, Massachusetts, *commissioned* songwriter Philip Greely to compose a song for the company. He titled the *jingle* "The Uncle Sam Shoe," and gave it a two-step beat so people could dance to the song, presumably while wearing their Uncle Sam shoes. The cover of the sheet music included a drawing of Uncle Sam and a lady friend, looking at the company's shoes.

Around the time Uncle Sam was recruiting soldiers for World War I, he was also selling oatmeal and pianos. In 1916, the Baldwin Piano Company ran advertisements showing Uncle Sam sitting at a Baldwin piano under the caption: "The Instrument He Was Born to Play." Two years later, the manufacturers of Cream of Wheat oatmeal advertised their company by picturing Uncle Sam holding aloft a steaming bowl of Cream of Wheat.

In 1922, Campbell's Soup published advertisements in national magazines showing Uncle Sam holding the two "Campbell's Kids" in his arms over the caption "The best-fed nation on Earth."

In 1937, Mobil Oil Company produced an advertisement proclaiming "Mobil Gasoline America's Favorite." Under the headline, a happy-go-lucky Uncle Sam stands in front of a Mobil gas pump, giving America the thumbs up signal. In 1952, Mobil's competitor, Sinclair Oil, had no qualms about using Uncle Sam in one of its advertisements, showing a smiling Uncle Sam declaring, "Sinclair Oil is Different!"

In 1943, the Piper Airplane Company published advertisements featuring the company's airplanes buzzing around a huge Uncle Sam hat and the caption: "Learn to Fly for Uncle Sam!"

Sometimes, companies weren't satisfied merely with one American symbol in their advertisements. In the early 1900s, James S. Kirk and Company, a soap maker in Chicago, Illinois, published advertisements that included an American bald eagle. The eagle was dressed as Uncle Sam, sitting in a rocking chair, while his wife, also an American bald eagle, washed his clothes using Kirk and Company soap. A similar effort was made in 1928 by Haig & Haig, which made whiskey. The advertisements published by Haig & Haig showed Uncle Sam tipping his hat to the Statue of Liberty, who held up a bottle of Haig and Haig whiskey instead of her torch.

Text-Dependent Questions

What was one of the first companies to use the image of Uncle Sam in its advertisements? What product was the company selling?

Research Project

Using the Internet, search for "Uncle Sam" and "advertising" to find some modern companies that use the image of Uncle Sam to promote their products. Print out three advertisements, and write a short paragraph about each describing how they portray the Uncle Sam image to create a positive attitude toward their product.

Words to Understand

anthem—a hymn or song, often celebrating patriotism.

pomp—a show of magnificence or splendor.

progenitor—the founder of a family or institution.

provisions—a supply of food or other necessary materials.

Yankee—originally "Jan Kee," a nickname for Dutch settlers in New York; eventually, the term was applied to all early Americans. It is now usually used to describe people from the New England region.

It is common to see stiltwalkers dressed as Uncle Sam towering over paraders on the Fourth of July and other holidays. Uncle Sam remains a symbol of the United States that is recognized around the world.

An Enduring Symbol

Uncle Sam's story may have started in the War of 1812, but he certainly wasn't the first imaginary character to serve as a symbol for Americans.

During the Revolutionary War, colonists sang about *"Yankee* Doodle." The British had unwittingly provided their colonists with that image—British soldiers would make fun of the backwoods Americans, calling them Yankee Doodles. Of course, when the Americans chased the British out of Concord, the colonists showed the British soldiers that Yankee Doodle was no dim country boy. In fact, the *Pennsylvania Journal* newspaper reported on May 24, 1775, that the British heard the song played as they retreated from Concord. "Since then, 'Yankee Doodle' sounds less sweet in their ears," the story said. The song became a favorite tune sung by Americans and played on their fifes and drums. "Yankee Doodle" also became an *anthem* of the Continental Army.

Americans never seemed to put a face on Yankee Doodle, although, as the song goes, he was known to wear a feather in his cap.

Another early symbol of America was "Brother Jonathan." Shortly after the start of the Revolutionary War, General George Washington is said to have been greatly concerned at the lack of ammunition and other *provisions* available to his soldiers. After meeting with his officers, Washington remarked, "We must consult Brother Jonathan on the subject." Who was Brother Jonathan? It was probably Jonathan Trumbull, the governor of Connecticut and Washington's close friend.

During the war, Brother Jonathan was a symbol of the ordinary soldier, ready to fight for liberty even though it meant little personal gain. He had common sense and good humor, and could not tolerate the *pomp* and self-importance most Americans associated with the British.

After the Revolution, there were continued references to Brother Jonathan in the newspapers, on the stage, and in song. This continued at least through the Civil War but, again, Americans failed to form an image of the symbol that would last through the ages. Today, Brother Jonathan is little-remembered.

So why has Uncle Sam remained a beloved symbol when Yankee Doodle and Brother Jonathan each eventually fell out of favor?

This cartoon from 1814 shows Brother Jonathan, an early symbol of the United States, confronting John Bull, the representation of Great Britain. Over time, the image of Uncle Sam replaced Brother Jonathan as a symbol of the U.S. government.

Certainly, James Montgomery Flagg's portrayal of Uncle Sam during a time of a great national crisis had a lot to do with his success. In times of war, Americans look toward a strong leader to guide them. It is likely that many Americans pictured their father's face in the strong features and granite expression exhibited by Uncle Sam in the Flagg recruiting poster.

In 1961, the citizens of Troy asked the U.S. Senate to recognize Sam Wilson as the inspiration for Uncle Sam. The Senate acted on Troy's request, and declared Sam Wilson the inspiration, or *progenitor*, for Uncle Sam.

Since then, the government has not hesitated to call on Uncle Sam whenever he is needed to fire up the spirit of Americans.

In 1998, the U.S. Postal Service placed Uncle Sam's image on a stamp. Two years later, the U.S. Department of Defense printed 200,000 new posters based on the Flagg image of Uncle Sam to help remind people of the sacrifices made by American servicemen and servicewomen. The image of Uncle Sam continues to be used on U.S. military recruiting posters today.

And so Uncle Sam has always been there for Americans. During the War of 1812, General Dearborn's soldiers knew they could rely on him for their suppers.

Today the U.S. Army still uses posters of Uncle Sam, such as this one in a recruiting center in New York's Times Square, to encourage young people to join the military.

He was there for the readers of *Harper's Weekly*, who looked to Uncle Sam for leadership. He has been there for America's wartime leaders, who relied on him to help recruit their soldiers.

> **Make Connections**
>
> Visitors to Troy, New York, will find a statue erected to honor Uncle Sam Wilson at Third and River streets; there is also a parking garage, natural foods store and bowling alley in Troy named after Uncle Sam.

"The tall, white-haired figure of Uncle Sam—his stern, sagacious face graced by a flowing beard, and his distinguished top hat adorned by stars and stripes—is a beloved symbol of the United States," former president George H.W. Bush once said. "Recognized around the world, the striking visage of Uncle Sam recalls the pride and strength of the American people, as well as the freedom we enjoy.

Text-Dependent Question
In what year was Sam Wilson officially recognized as the inspiration for the Uncle Sam character?

Research Project
Go a news source and identify a current event or issue that involves the U.S. government. Once you understand the issue, draw your own political cartoon, using Uncle Sam to represent the U.S. interest or approach to the subject. Use dialogue to make clear how Uncle Sam is reacting in your cartoon.

Chronology

1766 Sam Wilson born on September 13 in Menotomy, Massachusetts, to Edward and Lucy Wilson.

1775 On April 18, Paul Revere rides past the Wilson home on his way to warn the colonists about the British advance on Lexington and Concord.

1789 Sam Wilson and his brother Ebenezer settle in Troy, New York, where they work as brickmakers.

1793 The Wilson brothers establish E&S Wilson, a meatpacking company.

1813 E&S Wilson packs meat for soldiers camped near Troy; an employee of the company jokes that the "U.S." stamped on the barrels stands for "Uncle Sam." On September 7, a Troy newspaper makes the first published reference to Uncle Sam as a symbol of the United States.

1830 A newspaper cartoonist draws the first caricature of Uncle Sam.

1843 Clown Dan Rice, who would portray Uncle Sam for more than 30 years, gets his first circus job.

1854 Sam Wilson dies in Troy, New York, on July 31.

1870s *Harper's Weekly* cartoonist Thomas Nast begins to depict Uncle Sam as a white-whiskered gentleman in a star-spangled outfit.

1916 On July 6, the magazine *Leslie's Weekly* publishes a portrait of Uncle Sam by James Montgomery Flagg; the illustration is turned into a very popular U.S. Army recruiting poster.

1961 Congress recognizes Sam Wilson of Troy, New York, as the "progenitor of America's national symbol Uncle Sam."

Series Glossary of Key Terms

capstone—a stone used at the top of a wall or other structure.

cornerstone—the first stone placed at a spot where two walls meet, usually considered the starting point of construction.

dome—an element of architecture that resembles the hollow upper half of a sphere.

edifice—a large building with an imposing appearance.

facade—the decorative front of a building.

foundation—the stone and mortar base built below ground that supports a building, bridge, monument, or other structure.

hallowed—holy, consecrated, sacred, or revered.

keystone—the architectural piece at the crown of a vault or arch which marks its apex, locking the other pieces into position.

memorial—something designed to help people remember a person or event in history.

obelisk—a shaft of stone that tapers at the peak.

pantheon—a public building containing monuments to a nation's heroes.

pedestal—the base or support on which a statue, obelisk, or column is mounted.

portico—a roof supported by columns, usually extending out from a building.

rotunda—a large and high circular hall or room in a building, usually surmounted by a dome.

standard—a flag or banner that is adopted as an emblem or symbol by a nation.

symbol—an item that represents or stands for something else.

Further Reading

Foner, Eric. *Give Me Liberty!: An American History*. New York: W.W. Norton, 2011.

Goodwin, Doris Kearns. *The Bully Pulpit: Theodore Roosevelt, William Howard Taft, and the Golden Age of Journalism*. New York: Simon & Schuster, 2013.

Halloran, Fiona Deans. *Thomas Nast: The Father of Modern Political Cartoons*. Chapel Hill: University of North Carolina Press, 2012.

Hicks, Terry Allan. *Uncle Sam*. New York: Benchmark Books, 2009.

Meagher, Cecile Ann. *America's Favorite Uncle*. New York: Calm Productions, 1998.

Monroe, Tyler. *Uncle Sam*. North Mankato, Minn.: Capstone Press, 2013.

Suen, Anastasia. *Uncle Sam*. Illus. by Matthew Thomas Skeens. North Mankato, Minn.: Picture Window Books, 2008.

West, Delno C., and Jean M. West. *Uncle Sam and Old Glory: Symbols of America*. New York: Atheneum, 2000.

Internet Resources

http://www.city-of-troy.com/troywlsn.html

The city of Troy, New York, provides this page with history and genealogy of Sam Wilson, the progenitor of Uncle Sam.

http://www.loc.gov/exhibits/treasures/trm015.html

The Library of Congress exhibit "The Most Famous Poster," about James Montgomery Flagg's depiction of Uncle Sam, is part of the American Memory series.

http://www.thomasnast.com

Harper's magazine presents this website dedicated to the artwork of Thomas Nast, the 19th century political cartoonist who played a critical role in making the Uncle Sam image a popular symbol of the United States government.

http://www.usa.gov/visitors/about.shtml

This page provided by the U.S. government gives visitors an opportunity to learn about the United States of America, including links to information about patriotic symbols, American culture and history, government departments and agencies, and other interesting information.

Index

Anderson, Elbert, 18, 19
Arlington, Massachusetts, 9

Baldwin Piano Company, 34
Bellow, Frank H.T., 25
Berry Brothers, 33, 34
Boston, 11, 24, 34
British soldiers, 9–11, 17
"Brother Jonathan," 38, 39
Bunker Hill, battle of, 14
Bush, George H.W., 41

Calhoun, John, 17
Campbell's Soup, 34
Chapman, John "Johnny
    Appleseed," 14, 15
Civil War, 29, 38
Clay, Henry, 17
Concord, Massachusetts, 11, 14,
    37, 38
Continental Army, 14, 38
Cream of Wheat, 34

Dearborn, Henry, 17, 19–21, 40
Declaration of Independence, 23

E&S Wilson, 16, 19

Flagg, James Montgomery, 31, 39

Gay Nineties, 30
Gleason, Jonas W., 19–20
Greenbush, New York, 17, 19

Haig & Haig, 35

Harper's Weekly, 26, 27, 29, 41
Hudson River, 15, 16, 19

Independence Day, 13, 19
Industrial Revolution, 29–30

Jackson, Andrew, 24
James S. Kirk & Company, 35

Leslie's Weekly, 31
Lexington, Massachusetts, 10, 14
Lunenberg, Massachusetts, 14

Mann, Benjamin, 14
Mann, Betsey, 14, 16
Mason, New Hampshire, 14, 16
Medford Road, 9, 11
Menotomy, Massachusetts, 9, 10
Mobil Oil, 35

Nast, Thomas, 26–29
New York City, 16

Parker, John, 10
Percy, Hugh, 9, 10
Piper Airplane Company, 35

Revere, Paul, 9
Revolutionary War, 10, 15, 17, 37,
    38
Rice, Dan, 28, 29

Sinclair Oil, 35

Troy, New York, 14–17, 19, 20, 23,

Index

24, 39, 40
Trumbull, Jonathan, 38
Tsar Nicholas, 40

Uncle Sam
    Representations of, 24–31,
       33–35, 39
    Symbolism of, 13, 15, 23–31,
       39–41
Uncle Sam Shoemakers, 34
United States Army, 18, 21, 24, 31

Wapato Fruit and Cold Storage
    Company, 34
War Department, 31

War of 1812, 17, 23, 37, 40
Washington, George, 38
Wilson, Ebenezer, 14, 15
Wilson, Edward, 9, 11, 14
Wilson, Lucius, 21
Wilson, Lucy, 9, 14
Wilson, Samuel,
    as Uncle Sam, 13, 16–21, 37,
       40
    life of, 9, 11, 14–17, 20, 24, 40
Winthrop, Hannah, 11
World War I, 23, 30–31, 34

"Yankee Doodle," 37, 38, 39

Picture Credits

Contributors

BARRY MORENO has been librarian and historian at the Ellis Island Immigration Museum and the Statue of Liberty National Monument since 1988. *The Statue of Liberty Encyclopedia* (2000), *The Encyclopedia of Ellis Island* (2004), *Ellis Island's Famous Immigrants* (2008), and *The Ellis Island Quiz Book* (2011). He also co-edited a scholarly study on world migration called *Leaving Home: Migration Yesterday and Today* (2011). His biography has been included in *Who's Who Among Hispanic Americans*, *The Directory of National Park Service Historians*, *Who's Who in America*, and *The Directory of American Scholars*. Mr. Moreno lives in New York City.

HAL MARCOVITZ has written more than 100 books for young readers. He lives in Chalfont, Pennsylvania, with his wife, Gail. They have two grown daughters, Ashley and Michelle.